THE GULF:
FUTURE SECURITY
AND BRITISH POLICY

THE GULF:
FUTURE SECURITY
AND BRITISH POLICY

THE EMIRATES CENTER FOR STRATEGIC STUDIES AND RESEARCH

THE GULF: FUTURE SECURITY AND BRITISH POLICY

Published by
The Emirates Center for Strategic Studies and Research
PO Box 4567
Abu Dhabi
United Arab Emirates

e-mail: root@ecssr.ac.ae
http: //www.ecssr.ac.ae

Distributed by
Ithaca Press, an imprint of Garnet Publishing Ltd
8 Southern Court
South Street
Reading
RG1 4QS

ISBN 0 86372 260 1

First Edition

British Library Cataloguing-in-Publication Data
A catalogue record for this book is available from the British Library

Printed in Lebanon

The opinions expressed in this volume are those of the individual
contributors and do not necessarily reflect the views of the
Emirates Center for Strategic Studies and Research

The Emirates Center for Strategic Studies and Research

The Emirates Center for Strategic Studies and Research (ECSSR) is an independent research institution dedicated to the promotion of professional studies and educational excellence in the UAE, the Gulf and the Arab world. Since its establishment in Abu Dhabi in 1994, ECSSR has served as a focal point for scholarship on political, economic and social matters. Indeed, ECSSR is at the forefront of analysis and commentary on Arab affairs.

The Center provides a forum for the scholarly exchange of ideas by hosting conferences and symposia, organizing workshops, sponsoring a lecture series and publishing original and translated books and research papers. ECSSR also has an active fellowship and grant program for the writing of scholarly books and for the translation, into Arabic, of works relevant to the Center's mission. Moreover, ECSSR has a large library including rare and specialized holdings, and a state-of-the-art technology center, which has developed an award-winning website that is a unique and comprehensive source of information on the Gulf.

Through these and other activities, ECSSR aspires to engage in mutually beneficial professional endeavors with comparable institutions worldwide, and to contribute to the general educational and scientific development of the UAE.

Contents

Preface

Since 1997, the Emirates Center for Strategic Studies and Research (ECSSR) has organized a major annual conference on Gulf security, providing a unique opportunity for senior officials, scholars and policy makers to convene and address topics of significance to the Arabian Gulf region.

This publication is based on the proceedings of ECSSR's second annual Gulf Security: A National Perspective conference entitled, "The Gulf: Future Security and British Policy," held in London, April 29–30, 1998 and co-organized with Gulf Consultancy Services and the Royal United Services Institute for Defence Studies (RUSI). The volume contains a number of presentations delivered at the two-day event. Although the publication is not meant to be a holistic approach to Gulf security, it does shed light on some of the critical issues involved and offers an interesting insight into the views held by current British and Gulf defense policy makers.

By presenting the Gulf Security conference, ECSSR seeks to provide a framework for the discussion and development of common interests in the area of Gulf security. ECSSR's first conference entitled "Gulf Security: A National Perspective," held in Abu Dhabi in 1997, gathered senior officials and intellectuals from the Gulf Co-operation Council (GCC) states to debate key topics which included regional military threats, obstacles to socio-economic development and potential challenges to political stability. Participants stressed that although Gulf security and regional defense policy should be organized primarily within a national and regional framework, for an arrangement of this type to succeed, support and encouragement from allies would be essential. ECSSR recognizes the long-standing political and defense ties that exist between members of the GCC and the United Kingdom, and it is for this very reason that the theme of the second conference was chosen.

Conference Findings

Given the events of the past decade, the Gulf has clearly been identified as one of the world's most volatile regions. In light of the common interest of promoting Gulf security, the GCC and UK representatives strove to promote and nurture defense and security dialogue.

The two-day conference had three core objectives:

- to offer GCC and UK policy makers an opportunity to engage in open and informal discussions, exchange information, find solutions to problems and explore ideas and views relevant to the current and future security status of the Gulf region
- to allow conference participants from the United Kingdom to present results from the Strategic Defence Review, the country's comprehensive military policy plan, to GCC colleagues and to discuss with them, in an in-depth manner, its implications for the UK's policy vis-à-vis the Gulf
- to foster and forge closer security ties between the GCC states and the UK.

The participants agreed that the immediate threats to Gulf security are Iraq and Iran. Other threats to stability in the region include the lack of progress on the Middle East peace process. It was concluded, however, that not all threats to the region are external. It is important that social and economic policies pursued by Gulf countries sustain stability, and that a greater range of consultative mechanisms be developed. Unresolved and intractable boundary disputes also have potential for provoking conflict.

Finally, the impact of the Revolution in Military Affairs on Gulf security and the need to coordinate command and control mechanisms were discussed. Greater integration and cooperation by the GCC states was identified by the participants as a major factor in enhancing Gulf security.

Introduction

Dr. Jamal S. Al-Suwaidi

Gulf Security – A National Perspective II

On behalf of His Highness Lieutenant General Sheikh Muhammad Bin Zayed Al-Nahyan, Chief-of-Staff of the United Arab Emirates Armed Forces, it gives me great pleasure to welcome you to the second Gulf Security: A National Perspective conference entitled, "The Gulf: Future Security and British Policy."

At the outset, allow me to extend my sincerest gratitude to all the participants present here today, in particular, the Right Honourable George Robertson and the esteemed Ministers and Government Officials from the United Kingdom. My deepest appreciation also goes to His Highness Sheikh Salem Sabah Al-Salem Al-Sabah and Their Highnesses and Excellencies, the esteemed participants from the Gulf Co-operation Council (GCC) countries. It is precisely their participation in events such as this that paves the way for a constructive cooperation among all those who have a stake in the security of the Gulf region. It is the goal of this forum to encourage frank and objective discussion of Gulf security issues in the hope of reaching a more complete understanding of the current situation and thus promoting the goals of peace and stability throughout the region.

I would also like to extend my gratitude and appreciation to Mr. Geoffrey Tantum and Rear Admiral Richard Cobbold, Director of the Royal United Services Institute of Defence Studies (RUSI), as well as their respective staff, for the effort and support extended to the Emirates Center for Strategic Studies and Research (ECSSR) in preparing for this important meeting. We are grateful to all who have worked so hard to make this conference a reality.

The Emirates Center places particular importance on being able to provide a forum in which to analyze and examine relevant public policy issues. It is our mission to identify as well as to discuss the national security priorities of the Arab Gulf region. As such, we hope to broaden the understanding of and bring focus and enlightenment to frequently debated topics that are of critical importance to the Gulf region.

This gathering brings together senior representatives from the six GCC states and the United Kingdom in order to focus on the defense policies that are at the center of our relationship. It is important to realize that an effective Gulf security framework will only come to fruition when national and international defense policies are organized within a regional context. However, in order to reach and maintain this position, the support of long-standing allies is absolutely essential. This conference aims to lay the foundation from which closer security ties between the GCC states and the UK can be built.

The close connection between regional instability and the preservation of global security is nowhere more evident than in the Arabian Gulf region. This is because Gulf security is ultimately the result of the interaction among different yet interrelated factors. The complexity of the issue itself and the challenges that it presents to all those who deal with Gulf security are greatly enhanced by the fact that here national, regional and international interests overlap and often compete with each other. Furthermore, Gulf security involves political, economic and social aspects that directly and indirectly interact to produce a force that in turn requires a responsive and flexible public policy. Gulf security and stability is and will continue to be threatened by arms proliferation, ethnic and religious tensions, and the social and political dislocation associated with global economic change. The lingering repercussions of recent regional conflicts as well as the looming threat of additional military confrontations remain a stark reminder of the fragile stability and security of the area.

In assessing the current military security environment in the region, one needs to focus on three fronts. The first is the challenge that Iran and Iraq continue to represent towards the Arab Gulf states. The second is the establishment of collaborative efforts among all those states that have a concern in Gulf security. The third is the current security environment and the need to focus on steps to achieve a lessening of tensions in order to reduce the likelihood of a possible military confrontation. In this regard, the active participation of the GCC states in constructing a broader security paradigm is absolutely essential.

The end of the Cold War presents an opportunity to develop a more stable indigenous security paradigm that no longer needs to abide by the unofficial rules of a bipolar system. Such a solution has ultimately to involve all the countries of the Arabian Gulf. In addition, while effective military security remains of paramount importance, a greater degree of emphasis needs to be placed on economic prosperity as a stabilizing factor to establish vigorous and enduring economic and trade relations among the countries interested in maintaining Gulf security. A more interdependent environment needs to be created in order to give all states a stake in the preservation of peace. As a whole, the development of a sound and coherent GCC strategy, an effective public policy, the continuing evolvement of economic growth strategies and broader regional issues such as the Arab–Israeli conflict all have an enormous impact on Gulf security.

It is my hope that over the course of the next two days, each of us will gain a better understanding of the security issues that will carry the GCC–UK relationship into the next century. We must be aware that, together with the expectations of peace and prosperity, unforeseen challenges are harbored in this new era. It is therefore our task not only to define the present challenges and provide comprehensive responses to them but also to prepare the groundwork for future security challenges.

1

Welcome Address

Rt. Hon George Robertson MP

Your Highnesses, Your Excellencies, Ladies and Gentlemen. It is my privilege to welcome you all to London for this conference. His Highness Lieutenant General Sheikh Muhammad Bin Zayed Al-Nahyan, ECSSR, Mr. Geoffrey Tantum and the Royal United Services Institute are to be congratulated on bringing together such a distinguished gathering of policy makers and experts.

The security of the Gulf is vital to the United Kingdom's strategic and economic interests. Those who allege that our main interest lies in defense sales could not be more wrong. The security of the Gulf has figured prominently in our own Strategic Defence Review, the UK's military policy document. The Gulf has also, along with Bosnia, been at the center of the operational issues I have had to face since taking office.

Earlier in 1998, I took the very serious decision to deploy an aircraft carrier and Tornado bombers to the Gulf to demonstrate that the United Kingdom was not prepared to stand aside while Saddam Hussein defied the United Nations Security Council over his weapons of mass destruction. Happily, that particular crisis was resolved without resort to force, but I firmly believe that the decision by the United States, the United Kingdom and many other members of the international community to deploy forces to the Gulf was an important factor in persuading Saddam to back down at that point. As the UN Secretary General said in Baghdad, "you can do a lot more with diplomacy when it is backed up by firmness and force."

The potential for further conflict in the Gulf remains clear. Saddam Hussein has shown himself to be ruthless and untrustworthy. He has twice invaded his neighbors and has not only developed weapons of mass destruction but has made use of chemical weapons.

I should add that our quarrel is with Saddam Hussein and his regime, not with the Iraqi people. We have consistently sought to alleviate their suffering, often in the face of obstruction by Saddam Hussein. In early 1998, we sponsored Security Council Resolution 1153, which more than doubled the value of the "oil for food" arrangements. And in mid-April, 1998, we hosted in London a humanitarian meeting that brought together experts from the United Nations, the European Union (EU), donor countries and non-governmental organizations to consider how the plight of the Iraqi people can be eased.

There are aspects of Iranian policy too that continue to pose potential risks for the security and stability of the region and which need to be watched carefully, notwithstanding the more encouraging words we have been hearing recently from President Muhammad Khatami.

I am conscious too that the lack of progress in the Middle East Peace Process has a destabilizing impact on the Gulf. During my recent visit to Saudi Arabia and the United Arab Emirates (UAE), I was impressed by the strength of the arguments put to me on this score. We are sensitive to these views. This government has made the peace process one of the highest priorities for our EU Presidency, as demonstrated by the visits that Tony Blair and Robin Cook have made to the Peace Process countries. No one is under any illusions as to the difficulties that will need to be overcome to reinvigorate the Peace Process, but we remain ready to lend assistance where we can.

Of course not all threats to security are military in nature, nor is the use of force always the right response to a threat. As defense policy makers, we are naturally concerned to ensure that we have the policies and capabilities that enable us to cope in the most demanding circumstances; but I am also convinced that our armed forces have other significant parts to play in promoting stability and security. The existence of strong, well-equipped, well-trained and properly accountable armed forces is itself a deterrent against aggression. That deterrence will be all the greater if there is clear solidarity between the nation or nations under threat and their friends, both within and outside the region. That is one of the major lessons we in the United Kingdom learnt from the success of the North Atlantic Treaty Organization (NATO) in standing up to the threat of the Warsaw Pact for more than four decades.

Our service personnel also have a role to play in building trust and reducing the underlying causes of instability. Officers talking together or training together can be an effective way of shaping a peaceful security environment and the importance of this "defense diplomacy," as I term it, is one of the major themes of our Strategic Defence Review. I hope there may be scope for exploring the application of some of these ideas to Gulf security during the conference. It is an area where I believe the United Kingdom, which already has a significant training and advisory presence in the region, is well placed to help.

It is significant that this conference should be taking place in London. During the two visits I have made to the Gulf, I have been struck by the fact that the UK and the GCC states are bound together not only by common interests, but also by ties of history, understanding and affection. I myself have been received with great warmth and hospitality wherever I have been. I have been struck too, by the good relations that exist between our military personnel and by the generous support provided for UK forces in the Gulf. These links provide a firm foundation for continued cooperation on defense in the future.

The United States is of course central, both to underpinning Gulf security and to reinvigorating the Middle East Peace Process. But I believe that the United Kingdom also has a worthwhile role to play, both in its own right and as a trusted ally of the United States, an ally that is able to make a distinctive contribution to the formulation of policy in Washington.

In these opening remarks I have naturally given my own perspective on some of the issues the conference will be addressing. But I – and other representatives of Her Majesty's Government – very much look forward to hearing from our GCC friends about what they believe the major security problems they face will be and how the UK can assist in addressing them. We value the views of our friends and wish to take account of them in our own policy-making.

2

Gulf Security: UK Policy and Implications of the Strategic Defence Review

Dr. John Reid MP

This Government was elected in May 1997, committed to ensuring that Britain plays a leadership role internationally and to underpinning this with strong defense. We are determined to contribute to wider international peace and security in conjunction with our allies.

Peace and security in the Gulf are of great importance to the United Kingdom because of our strategic, economic and commercial interests in the region, because of the presence of our sizable expatriate communities, and because of the close historical and personal contacts between the United Kingdom and the Gulf. We value these links greatly, and this government seeks actively to maintain them. I therefore welcome the opportunity to participate in this conference and to say a few words about UK policy in the region and the implications of the Strategic Defence Review, Britain's defense policy document.

Our objectives in the Gulf are forward looking; we seek long-term peace and stability, not just to avert the next crisis. We aim for a point in the future where all the countries in the region recognize international norms of behavior. Although we may be pulling back from the brink of a conflict at this moment, there is clearly a long way to go before reaching this endstate.

The Strategic Defence Review, which we began after taking office and is now in its final stages, is vital to the achievement of our long-term aims since it will give clarity and cohesion to our defense planning, and a long-term vision for defense well into the next century.

For our friends and allies, in the Gulf and elsewhere, this will be welcoming and reassuring. The Strategic Defence Review is unlike some previous exercises of this kind in that it is foreign policy led, not resource-driven. It is not therefore a cost-cutting exercise but a genuine strategic re-examination of Britain's interests, commitments and responsibilities.

It has become commonplace to say that the world in which we pursue these interests, commitments and responsibilities has been transformed in the past decade. This is, however, the first time we have been able to think through the implications of the end of the Cold War and events such as the Gulf conflict and the crises in the former Yugoslavia, with an eye on the longer-term as well as immediate problems.

From a purely British perspective, our security has been vastly improved during this period. But the benefits have not been shared equally, and we still face the challenge of instability in Europe, which, if left unaddressed, could spread and risk the re-creation of a major external military threat. Beyond Europe, we have wide international interests and a major stake in world peace and stability. As a permanent member of the United Nations Security Council, we have a responsibility to play an active and, where appropriate, a leadership role in international security.

Of course, our interests do not extend equally everywhere. Europe and the North Atlantic Treaty Organization (NATO) must be a priority. Beyond Europe, we believe that our interests are most likely to be directly affected by events in the Gulf, the Near East and North Africa. This does not mean that the Review will lead to our re-creating a military capability "East of Suez." That would be a retrograde step. But it does mean that the Review has confirmed the importance of the Gulf region to British economic interests, the value of our bilateral ties with Gulf states and the importance of our wider UN responsibilities in the Gulf area. We must therefore be ready to respond, in combination with others, to support stability when it is threatened in the Gulf.

This is not simply rhetoric. We gave a clear example of our willingness to act in our response to the crisis in Iraq in early 1998. And I made clear in my speech during the Defence Debate in the House of Commons in October 1997 that our interests and obligations in Europe, the Mediterranean and the Gulf would primarily determine the size and shape of our Armed Forces.

I expect the Strategic Defence Review to introduce radical change in some key areas of defense. Our aim, to produce modern forces for the modern world, requires us to take the long view. I would expect these changes to meet with support from others with an interest in the Gulf and its security.

These changes will have implications for the structure and readiness of our forces and our ability to project force. In the future, our forces will need the ability to deploy to meet the more diverse challenges we face. We must be able to go to the crisis, rather than expect the crisis to come to us.

The Joint Rapid Deployment Force (JRDF), created in 1996 to provide the UK with a joint force ready to respond to a broad range of crises wherever they arise, was a step in the right direction. But, for it to be properly effective, it needs enhanced transport and logistic support, together with greater firepower and better command and control. The Review addresses all these points. We also need to break down the potentially divisive and militarily inappropriate distinction the JRDF drew between forces for NATO and forces for other tasks. All of this will give us much more capable Joint Rapid Reaction Forces, from which we will be able to deploy carefully tailored packages of forces, at short notice, anywhere in the world.

Our objective in the Strategic Defence Review is to produce modern, flexible, high-capability forces to underpin our foreign and security policy, with equipment and technology that gives them a decisive battle-winning edge. Our Armed Forces will continue to make a distinctive, high-quality contribution to multinational operations, supporting international stability and security in the Gulf and elsewhere.

We will produce strong defense for the twenty-first century and ensure that Britain remains a force for good. We will also continue to support those who are not able to counter the threat themselves. In 1991, through consultation and a unified approach against Saddam Hussein, the international coalition was able to defeat the fourth largest army in the world. Since the Gulf War, the United Kingdom's security links with the Gulf Co-operation Council (GCC) states have increased. We have signed or are in the process of negotiating a number of defense accords which provide for increased cooperation in a range of defense activities.

The United Kingdom's military presence in the region has also remained at a higher level than before and includes the Armilla vessels, the No-Fly Zone patrols, substantial numbers of personnel on load services, regular exercise programs and visits by specialist training teams. The UK military contribution to the western presence in the region underpins the United Kingdom's political commitment to security in the Gulf. It is also a reflection of our broader responsibilities as a member of the Security Council.

One of the themes of this conference is improving cooperation and recognizing the importance of working together, and so I naturally support efforts to improve cooperation within the Gulf Co-operation Council. Our own experiences in NATO and within the Gulf have proven that we and our allies are more likely to form an effective deterrent if we stand shoulder to shoulder.

From the outset, the United Kingdom has been an enthusiastic supporter of the Gulf Co-operation Council. We encourage a strong and cohesive body with collective policies and defense capability. Cooperation in the field of defense is the principal means by which the members can manage threats against their own security and play a vital part in regional stability.

I would like to congratulate GCC members on the development of their armed forces, both in numbers and capability of equipment, and the skills and knowledge of military personnel. However, I would suggest that in the current security environment, Western military support and a Western military presence in the region are also important.

The key to deterring aggression is diplomacy backed up by the credible threat of force. Primarily, this deterrence means US military might. However, there is a distinct and important role for the United Kingdom to play in both political and military terms. Our contribution is welcomed not least by the United States, which recognizes our willingness to share the burden. This has given us insight into the US decision-making process and allowed us to influence US security policy.

The United Kingdom can also support the development of Gulf Co-operation Council forces by the provision of training and advice and by the supply of high quality and proven defense equipment. This is an area where traditionally the United Kingdom has been able to make a contribution and where we remain willing to provide assistance. As George Robertson said earlier, these activities fit in well with our ideas about making greater use of our Armed Forces for defense diplomacy.

We also welcome the opportunity for UK forces to train in the Gulf. Exercises demonstrate our capability to deploy to and operate in the region and therefore add to deterrence. The effect is enhanced through combined exercises with our GCC allies, which support the development of GCC forces and the ability of our forces to operate together.

The focus of this conference is Gulf security, and I am sure that much will be said about Iraq. There is no doubt that Saddam Hussein remains the major immediate threat to stability in the Gulf. In 1990, he demonstrated his ambitions to dominate the region, and he has on numerous occasions and in various ways shown that he is a threat to his neighbors. We are still waiting for Saddam Hussein to produce the evidence we need to be sure that he has destroyed all his weapons of mass destruction. Until the work of the UN Special Commission is complete, we believe that Saddam remains a threat to both regional and international peace. As we showed in the early-1998 crisis, we will not allow Saddam to defy the will of the international community by his resolute disregard for United Nations Security Council Resolutions. The authority of the United Nations must be upheld. And, although it is issues relating to weapons of mass destruction that make the front pages of the newspapers in the United Kingdom, we remember that there are a range of issues on which Saddam still has to supply satisfactory answers, prominent among these the fate of the missing Kuwaitis.

While I recognize that some were opposed to the use of military force, we believed that this was the only way that Saddam could be brought into line if he refused to comply with the wishes of the international community or chose to defy the will of the United Nations further. We have long known that Saddam only respects diplomacy when it is backed by credible military force, which is why we sent a carrier and despatched an air group to the Gulf in January, 1998, followed by the deployment of RAF Tornados to Kuwait. The credit for the successful outcome to the crisis needs to be shared by all who supported this policy and we are grateful to all who supported – and continue to support – these deployments.

As a defense minister, you may expect me to focus on the part the military force or, more accurately, the threat of military force has played in containing Iraq, but this is of course only one of the tools at our disposal. Economic measures through the imposition of sanctions have also played a part; but I recognize that sanctions have enabled Saddam to manipulate the truth and claim a propaganda victory in saying that our policies are leading to the deaths of innocent Iraqi children. Nothing could be further from the truth. The UK Government has no argument with the Iraqi people. You will know that we hosted a meeting last week to look at ways of improving the implementation of the "oil-for-food" scheme and ensuring that its revenues are spent on helping the Iraqi population who have already suffered for too long under Saddam's brutal regime.

So what about the future? We believe that for the foreseeable future, there is no realistic alternative to a policy of containment. Our longer-term objective is to see the reintegration of Iraq as a law-abiding member of the international community. We look forward to the day when Iraq will be a country with which trade and normal contacts will be possible. But this will not be possible until Iraq complies in full with Security Council resolutions and ceases to pose a threat to regional and international security.

Around April 1997, many – including myself – were concerned that the greatest long-term threat to Gulf security came from Iran. But is this still the case following the unexpected election of President Muhammad Khatami in 1997? We are certainly encouraged by the reforms that President Khatami is introducing. Iran's ratification of the Chemical Weapons Convention, its attempts to reduce tension with its neighbors and the West, and Iranian condemnation of terrorist attacks in Egypt and Algeria are all encouraging and very much a step in the right direction. In light of this, the European Union (EU) has decided to resume the EU–Iran dialogue suspended following the Mykonos Verdict in March 1997. But please be assured that we have not forgotten the past and are not naive. While President Khatami is good news for Iran and the region as a whole, there are Iranian policies that remain unacceptable. Through the European Union, we will continue to maintain pressure on Iran about its attempts to acquire weapons of mass destruction and its record of support for terrorism. We have made an approach; the future of this relationship rests with Iran's response and its willingness to address our concerns. Together we will watch Iran's moves closely and with interest.

George Robertson acknowledged the force of the argument that the lack of progress in the Middle East Peace Process made it more difficult to secure support for Western policies in the Gulf. This government is fully and actively committed to the search for a just and lasting peace and to promoting the development of the Palestinian areas through our aid program. One of the priorities for our EU presidency has been to ensure that the EU continues to play an active role, both seeking to support US efforts and pursuing complementary EU activity that is visible and credible. We and our EU partners have been working hard to establish a firm basis for progress. The US role of course remains central. But the EU stands ready to lend whatever assistance may be needed.

These are difficult issues, and I do not expect to have persuaded you that our policies are right in all respects. But I hope that I have at least reassured you that the issues of Gulf security are important to the UK and that after the conclusion of the Strategic Defence Review we will continue to work closely with our friends in the Gulf to tackle these issues and to contribute to the peace and security of the region.

3

Future Warfare: Implications for Gulf Defense

General Sir Charles Guthrie

I am delighted to have the opportunity to address this important conference on the subject of future warfare and the implications for defense in the Gulf region. I think the move towards globalization (i.e., the increase in economic, cultural and military links that bind countries) means that changes in future warfare will affect us all in similar ways, and not separately in the Gulf region.

In this context, I had hoped that I might be able to say more about the outcome of our Strategic Defence Review, as the thinking behind our plans for the future of the UK Armed Forces is relevant to the subject of this session, but I can add little to what we have heard already from Dr. Reid. Nevertheless, much of what I shall say is conditioned by the extensive debates that have taken place during our Review over the past ten months.

These are the five key areas for the future:

- the wide spectrum of potential conflicts
- the importance of the joint environment
- the need to have forces with deployability, including logistical support
- the benefits – and limitations – of new technology.
- the importance of interoperability with allies

This is a broad canvas and I cannot cover every aspect of these areas in the time available, but I hope I can raise some points to stimulate debate.

Spectrum of Conflict

The world is in many respects more complex and unpredictable than ten years ago. The fragmentation which has followed the end of the Cold War has refocused us on localized conventional war, and the spectrum of types of conflict that may occur is broad. At one end of the scale is a major war, such as the 1990–91 Gulf War; at the other is a small terrorist action. Of course, the Gulf War was high intensity in terms of hardware and force levels, while it was nevertheless brought to a conclusion relatively quickly and with few casualties on our side. This may not be the model for the future. There is also a trend towards multinational peace-keeping operations to which the community of responsible nations will wish to contribute. There is now an emphasis on what we call defense diplomacy (training teams and other activities that reinforce stability), but military forces will continue to need to be trained to cover the full scale of conflict. Because high-intensity fighting is very demanding, considerable resources will continue to be required for this sort of training. However, some reductions in field training are now possible through better simulation and computer-assisted exercises. Simulation is particularly important for exercising commanders who otherwise are taken up with the myriad practicalities and problems of exercising troops.

Whatever the intensity of the conflict, a trend that is worrying is the increasing probability of the use of chemical or, even worse, biological weapons. This, of course, lies at the heart of our continuing concerns with the Iraqi regime. Unfortunately, the technology of biological warfare (BW) is relatively simple for trained scientists and a country or organization can produce a credible weapon at low cost (but not at low risk). In asymmetric conflicts (i.e., conflicts where one participant is much more powerful in conventional military means), this could redress the balance of power. However, the means of effective delivery are rather harder to develop than the weapons. This increases the likelihood that chemical or biological attacks would be unconventional (i.e., delivered by special forces or terrorism, rather than by missile, aircraft or projectile). There does not seem much point, for example, in enormous expenditure on ballistic missile defense if the most likely means of delivery is a suitcase. All this points to the need for sound intelligence on chemical and biological weapons, and for military forces (and the civil population?) to have appropriate detection and force protection equipment.

Joint Environment

Next, it is clear that nearly all campaigns in the future will be joint in that they will involve all of the environments: sea, land and air. The Gulf region could hardly exemplify this point more perfectly in view of its geography. Each arm of the services needs to retain its own identity and ethos, but each must form part of an integrated whole on operations.

This carries implications for the organization and training of defense forces. Single-service leadership and organization is still fundamental, but defense organizations need a strong central control of resources to ensure that the balance between the environments, i.e., joint projects, is appropriately funded. Operations also need to be centrally directed – our own Permanent Joint Headquarters, separate from the Ministry of Defence Headquarters, may not be an exact model for other nations but it has got us off to an excellent start, and I firmly believe that the joint aspect does point the way ahead. When more than one service provides identical or very similar functions, rationalization is required to avoid a waste of resources. In addition, training is required that builds at each level, from the single-service competencies through to joint exercises involving front-line units and headquarters staff.

Deployability and Logistics

The major change for the North Atlantic Treaty Organization (NATO) has been the move from a static environment in Europe to a far more fluid and flexible environment where the one certainty is that we shall have to move to the area of the conflict. This is relatively simple for naval forces, provided resupply ships or host nation ports are available, but it is far harder for both air and land forces which carry a considerable "tail" of support. The lessons we have learnt recently have been in deployability and sustainability.

The first, deployability, is perhaps on the face of it less relevant to Gulf States, but of course the distances within the region are vast, and long-range movement of forces in any conflict would probably be necessary. Aircraft cannot provide the amount of lift required except for early entry or light forces, so the majority will have to move on land or sea. All countries will have to consider their new requirements; for the UK, we will certainly have to invest more in strategic lift, balancing the investment between air and sea elements. We also have to ensure that, when deployed, we can communicate effectively, and the demand for strategic communications – voice and data traffic, and probably video-conferencing – increases each year.

Secondly, forces must be sustainable when they are deployed, and this means providing flexible transport and distribution networks. This is resource and manpower intensive, and we have found that we must allocate more to this area if our front-line forces are to be fully combat capable. I recognize that there are differing levels of support depending on the intensity of the conflict, the context may not lend itself to high technology weapons, e.g., in the fight against terrorism or insurgents. Furthermore, increasing complexity means a potential increase in individual technical education and training and in collective training. Without investment in training, there is a risk of not being able to exploit fully the advantages of new technology.

New Technology

In terms of the benefits of new technology, one of the striking aspects has been the change in the lead from military to civil technology. The military has traditionally been the spearhead of progress, but there is now a civil lead in many areas, especially in computing and communications.

There is also a change in civil procurement and support methods, which will keep costs down and get equipment in service quicker (the rapid pace of change requires a quicker procurement cycle), but civil standards and methods are not always appropriate. "Off the shelf" may not be enough to win. Sometimes the "best" technology rather than merely "good" is required; "just-in-time" is not sound military logistics in war.

The ability to attack precisely at long range with far less vulnerability for the attacker will markedly increase. Also, the number of people required in military forces may be reduced due to precision-guided weaponry and automation, e.g., in unmanned air vehicles. But, conversely, peace-keeping operations are human resource intensive.

The information/decision cycle will decrease if the full power of modern command and control communications are employed. This should enable us to get inside the operational cycle of the opposition, but it also places pressure on our own commanders and there may be increased vulnerability to information warfare.

Interoperability

Finally, there is a need to keep up with allies. In the United States – a market leader, because it has major technology programs across the entire defense spectrum – many believe in a Revolution in Military Affairs based on information systems and precision weapons. I would prefer to call it an evolution, not a revolution. However, new minimum standards will inevitably be set (particularly in anything that involves computing power, such as command and control and communications systems). But constraints are likely on many nations' ability to keep up with the United States, first on cost grounds and second because there will be limits on technology transfer. Paradoxically, this is likely to limit the adoption of new technology by the United States, because if nobody can work with them, their ability to take part in coalitions would also be hampered.

4

Trends in GCC
Defense Cooperation

HH Sheikh Salem Sabah
Al-Salem Al-Sabah

The world has experienced, since the end of World War II, breathtaking changes and shifts in international relations, the reasons for and results of which are numerous. Many of these relations were violent conflicts, often escalating into full-scale wars. As a result of these conflicts, the world has sustained a large number of casualties which far exceeds the number of lives lost in both world wars. Wise politicians and determined decision makers worldwide have never ceased their efforts to replace conflict with entente, and to defuse destructive rivalries. The international community created bodies, such as the United Nations and its various agencies, and gave them the mandate to play the diplomatic and legal roles necessary for the settlement and resolution of these conflicts. The United Nations was also provided with mechanisms for international intervention and deterrent capabilities in order to avert these conflicts and defeat aggressors. These efforts enjoy the outright support of the superpowers, whose interests lie in the consolidation of world security. There are three phenomena that represent the most important types of international disputes:

- conflicts over sovereignty
- conflicts resulting from skepticism and mutual feelings of threat
- internal disputes that spill over and consequently jeopardize regional stability.

The Arab world is not an exception. It has witnessed tremendous conflicts and wars as a result of these three phenomena, often far exceeding the international ratio. The cost in human lives and material losses witnessed by the Middle East is much more than it could possibly afford at the expense of its people's aspirations for development. These conflicts have left behind tremendous human losses and pain from which we are still suffering.

The occupation and liberation of Kuwait constituted a new and unprecedented chapter in regional relations. It was also a new chapter, as a collective effort was made to defeat the Iraqi aggressor who, obsessed by war and expansionism, violated all Arab norms, agreements and conventions, including the Arab League Regional Charter and the Arab Joint Defense Agreement, which were originally designed to avert conspicuous regional conflicts.

The occupation and liberation of Kuwait also forged a broad Arab and international alliance of countries dedicated to peace and security, and determined to uphold the legitimacy of existing states and to stand up to flagrant aggression. Furthermore, the mechanisms of the United Nations and the concept of international law were engaged to deter the aggressor. Thus we came, as a result of the Kuwaiti experience, face to face with a new three-pronged equation for defending peace and avoiding war:

- Those countries rife with domestic violence, tension and oppression are the same countries that launch aggression and war in an attempt to avoid fulfilling their legal requirements. The most conspicuous example is Iraq.
- Peace-loving nations that uphold sovereignty join forces during times of crisis and defend the victims against the oppressors. This position was adopted by the Gulf Co-operation Council (GCC) countries, led by the Kingdom of Saudi Arabia, as well as the member states of the Damascus Declaration, namely Egypt and Syria, along with other Arab and peace-loving countries in the developing world.
- The international community, led by the most powerful countries which play leading roles in the UN Security Council, have not only important legal and political commitments to fulfill but also a real partnership to sustain with the purpose of defeating the aggressor and denying him the opportunity to benefit from the use of brutal force.

These three dimensions should be understood against a background so important to the state of Kuwait. Since the discovery of its oil resources, Kuwait has pursued a balanced policy of distributive development at the local and regional levels. Through a number of institutions, notably the Kuwait Fund for Arab Development, development projects for the Arab world have been designed to address population welfare issues and to broaden and strengthen the bonds of friendship throughout the world. Kuwait has adopted domestic policies that envisage a comprehensive strategy for development in economics, civil society and education. Moreover, Kuwait has introduced a modern constitution which allows its citizens to have a substantial input into the administration of their society. All these factors led to a united community loyal to its legitimate leadership, making it possible to defeat the Iraqi aggression against Kuwait in a manner unprecedented in form and substance, despite the magnitude and ferocity of the aggression.

These are the lessons drawn from our experiences. We believe that lasting security in the region must be based on:

- actual internal partnership
- a comprehensive plan for development
- an effective and balanced regional partnership
- broad friendship based on mutual respect and an international commitment to advancing economic and development issues.

We believe that this foundation is essential for smaller countries, the Arab region and the international community.

From this standpoint, we believe that a partnership with our brothers in the Gulf is essential, as the hostilities and conflicts surrounding us will not dissipate as long as territorial ambitions and domestic tensions remain in place. The deterrent force maintained in the Gulf, according to the Kuwaiti view, depends on this trio: stability and local development; military partnership for deterrent purposes; and an international coalition that recognizes common interests and goals.

Concentrating Power

Human resources are most important when facing security, political and development challenges – current or potential – in our region. The need to train people and mobilize their potential is extremely pressing for the Gulf. Well-trained personnel can be used to implement developmental programs and to protect the country through defense and security mechanisms. The task of producing qualified people becomes increasingly difficult when ever-changing technology necessitates a more advanced citizenry, fully aware of its national mission. Therefore, the most important challenge we face is the education and training of individuals. It is a social mission in which cultural leaders, educators and all segments of society are involved. Taking into account the relatively low population rates of the GCC countries compared to the large populations of other societies, human resource development is growing in importance; the urgency of this task, entrusted to planners and educators, becomes augmented.

Furthermore, the resources of our societies, no matter how abundant, will remain less than adequate, in view of regional circumstances. It is necessary to distribute these revenues on different fields that are indispensable for the efficient structure to which societies aspire. Therefore, the allocation of resources to achieve a balance between ambitions and capabilities is a burden we face not only on a daily basis but every time we try to achieve a balance between resources and national challenges and aspirations, especially with the growing need for socially conscious, well-trained human beings.

Benefitting from Resources of Strength

The elements that contribute to a powerful Gulf region are abundant. They stem from the intensified efforts exerted by our leaders and founding fathers and are due to their prudence and dedication. The political will of GCC leaders to keep this volatile part of the world free of futile rivalries, and to deal with international and regional innovations and effective developments and influences through a collective performance that maintains the common interests, is present. The recent initiative, proposed by His Highness Sheikh Jabber Al-Sabah, Amir of the State of Kuwait, and adopted by the GCC countries, calls for the establishment of a consultative popular assembly (*Al-Shoura*) to assist the institution of the Gulf summit. With its advice and opinions, this assembly promises to foster real confidence, along with the creation of *Al-Shoura* consultative bodies in their different formulas, intended to allow citizens the right to participate in GCC work and to shoulder their share of the responsibility in the country's defense. Military cooperation among the GCC member states is also one of the council's most advanced and coordinated activities. The GCC countries have numerous common strengths, including social origin, language, culture, traditions and customs, harmony in political and legal structure and in improving education systems. The GCC countries enjoy political stability due to the wise policies of their leaders. The GCC also maintains good foreign relations and its presence is appreciated regionally and internationally.

GCC Defense Cooperation

Since its establishment in 1981 in an atmosphere of regional turbulence, the GCC has made an intensive effort to achieve the best possible level of coordination on Gulf issues. The GCC leaders and nationals alike consider this regional body a catalyst for joint Arab action that will provide support for achieving the goals of the Islamic countries and all peace-loving nations. Consequently, it has become the hope for the future development of the region. The GCC has lent firm support to the implementation of UN Security Council resolutions intended to boost international peace and detente. It has also acted with the Arab League as well as the United Nations and its various agencies to support health, environmental and humanitarian policies. The "joint Gulf action" was the target that the Council has always tried to achieve in order to realize the highest degree of interaction and coordination among its members at both the popular and official levels.

In the military sphere, the GCC has set objectives related to the external security of its members:

- collective protection of the region's security and stability
- keeping the Gulf region out of international conflicts
- participation in the efforts to resolve international disputes
- providing the United Nations with the opportunity to play an essential and effective role, obeying its resolutions and approaches.

The GCC is based on a number of principles, the most important of which are the following:

- to assert the principle of good neighborliness as a rule by which the GCC member states will abide in their international dealings
- to respect the sovereignty of existing states and to emphasize and exercise non-interference in the domestic affairs of other countries
- to take the principle of peaceful cooperation as the cornerstone of world peace and security
- to support all attempts made to bring peace throughout the world.

GCC Military Strategy

Based on the mutual vision and understanding of the GCC states, a strategic perspective has been established. Taking into account the realities of size, human and material capabilities and the need to strike a balance between interests and common objectives, the GCC countries have defined their concept of defense and formulated their defense policy according to a well-defined system with a coherent framework that interacts with events and develops according to changes in the political and military environment.

The defense system of the GCC member states was designed to deal with acts of aggression according to the strategy described below. In the beginning, there will be full reliance on indigenous defensive capabilities including all supporting operations. Our countries are working hard to upgrade military and defensive capabilities to confront any possible threat, introducing all requirements for preparing the theater of operations and arrangements for general mobilization, in addition to the necessary preparation of forces and ancillary services. At the same time, appropriate measures are being taken to activate a smooth transition to the next phase.

In the next phase of the defense system, the activation and operation of the GCC collective defense mechanism will begin. All potential and capability will be channeled to implement what we have unanimously agreed upon. Action will be taken to confront the threat collectively according to agreed and predefined concepts and visions. It is not a secret that annual land, air and naval maneuvers, which are staged by selected units of the GCC armies, are basically intended to achieve full integration and common understanding if the need arises, as dictated by emerging circumstances.

These measures of military coordination among GCC member states have been gaining momentum for a long time. The idea was born at the beginning with the formation of the "Peninsula Shield Force" as the nucleus for movement towards joint and integrated military action which proved its wisdom and effectiveness in a practical manner during the military operations of Desert Storm and the liberation of Kuwait. Success resulted from the use of common grounds and unified conceptions.

The implementation of these measures continued in order to identify and thus avoid defects and shortcomings and to recognize the aspects of strength in order to enforce them. More practical and ambitious ideas were then introduced, through the continued meetings of the concerned military personnel at the GCC General Secretariat to upgrade that force and increase its efficiency so as to become a practical and active nucleus in the training and coordination of the envisioned unified Gulf army.

The third level in the Gulf defense system is the Arab level. The desire is still strong and the trend is still alive to boost the Arab role and revive the joint Arab Defense Agreement, which was violated and destroyed by the Iraqi regime. The Damascus Declaration was a clear indicator on the part of Gulf countries to keep the Arab defense spirit alive, and develop it at the regional level in order to maintain collective security.

The fourth level of the Gulf defense system supports the United Nations. With a view to preserving world peace and security, this level of the system tends to strengthen ties with the United Nations as well as alliances with friendly countries that also believe in the importance of maintaining peace in the interests of the region, its peoples and the world at large.

In this final context, Kuwait played host to a number of meetings, conferences and joint exercises with GCC member states, along with Egypt and Syria, with the United States, Britain, France and other countries acting as supervisors. During the exercises, code-named "Ultimate Resolve," concrete goals were realized which include the achievement of common coordination and a vision towards collective action. These render the political execution of the GCC defensive process capable of being implemented, and link it successfully to the regional and international systems.

Current and Potential Threats

The Gulf region is an environment of potential conflict. Social, political and economic turmoil contribute to the instigation of wars and violence. I have already made clear our undoubted resolve to upgrade our defense capabilities, both in Kuwait and at the GCC level in collaboration with our Arab neighbors and friendly countries, for the continued maintenance of peace and security. The Middle East region is still volatile. We must be constantly prepared to encounter any sudden outburst. This is an arduous and ever-changing process which demands full awareness and cooperation on the part of us all.

The stalemated peace process in the Middle East causes concern to the region and exhausts some of its best energies. It is a problem that annoys us all in the Gulf and the Arab world as well. It also causes concern for the West. But the biggest threat – and the most imminent danger – comes from the repeated aggression of Iraq, which neither believes in nor abides by conventions, agreements or the spirit and letter of international and regional laws. Iraq entered two destructive wars in less than two decades, in which it used weapons of mass destruction against its neighbors and its own people, killing thousands. It has also interfered in the internal affairs of many countries. Furthermore, its prisons still hold hostages from Kuwait and other countries, whom its troops had kidnapped from mosques, houses and the streets of Kuwait, for no apparent reason.

Iraq explicitly and regularly demonstrates its aggressiveness, shame-lessly celebrating every year the anniversary of its aggression on our country. Iraq also conceals highly lethal biological and chemical weapons, and routinely provokes the world community. In our opinion, this is the clear, direct and standing threat, not only against the State of Kuwait, but also to the stability of the entire region.

On another level, our brothers in the United Arab Emirates are faced with a complicated political situation regarding its occupied islands. It is a problem inherited from two previous regimes, the British and the Shah of Iran. The Gulf states are trying to explain to their Muslim neighbor Iran, especially under its new and moderate leadership, the importance of reaching a peaceful and just solution to this complicated problem which is consuming much of the resources of the two countries. Peoples in the Gulf found the recent Iranian diplomatic overtures very promising. We hope they will strive to promote peace and security of the Gulf and the welfare of all peoples of the region.

Conclusion

The trends in GCC defense represent a process of constant evolution and are subject to changes. Its pillars are deeply rooted in the political harmony that binds these Arab countries, their shared history, social origin, culture, language and common destiny. Their defense policy is based on a system of social, economic, political and military balance in which reliance on its human resources is the prime source and the first line of defense. Its political target is to settle disputes and rivalries through the authority of international law and to function only within its principles.

Those responsible for defense affairs in the Gulf, in line with their leaders' directives, spare no effort to achieve the following:

- coordination and planning
- consultation and follow-up on defense and security matters
- maintenance of regional peace and safety
- modernizing and upgrading of strategic weaponry to cope with international change
- development of national and collective defense policies.

The above is done in a manner that fulfills the common objectives of our countries and deals with the practical requirements of those policies, according to a unified and shared vision. Utilization of the defense agreements signed by some of the Gulf countries and certain big powers serves the Gulf collective defense system in a way that achieves the common goals of those countries.

The partnership we look for with our allies in the West is far greater than the supply of equipment. Nonetheless, we aspire to a partnership characterized by political and pragmatic understanding as well as by joint efforts in economic development and technology transfer.

We live in an era when the world prepares to bid farewell to the century of classic communications and embrace the age of telecommunications and information systems. It is an age that will be built by brilliant minds, which will create qualitative superiority – the dream of every leader – in order to achieve the difficult balance arising from the limited manpower base and the expanding elements of threat. In this vital and broad context, we look to our friends for assistance and counselling in order to achieve the noble objective of stability in our region and the advancement of our peoples.

The lesson we have drawn from the disaster of the aggression against us and the occupation and liberation of our country underlines the need for self-reliance in order to build a balanced, democratic society and distinguished Gulf relationships, along with interactive Arab and international relations.

Along these lines, we can build peace and cooperation to serve the best interests of the coming generations, and we can leave our country as it was left to us by our fathers and grandfathers – a land of peace, productivity and friendship.

5

Human Rights Issues
and British Policy

Lady Olga Maitland

His Highness Sheikh Salem Al-Sabah touched very briefly on an issue that sears the soul of every household in Kuwait. I refer to the 605 Kuwaitis who were captured during the Iraqi occupation in 1990-91. Iraqi soldiers removed them from their homes, their beds, the streets, their cars and even raided mosques. These citizens were men ranging in age from teenagers to 70-year-olds and included students, businessmen, civil servants and retired people.

Seven women were also abducted. All were taken to prisons in Iraq. One girl, taken at age 14, was hurled back across the border, having become totally deranged after suffering six years of systematic ill-treatment, torture and appalling abuse.

To many, the numbers may not seem that significant, but to a nation with a population of 1.5 million, it hurts every single family. In proportionate terms, their numbers represent the equivalent of a quarter of a million American citizens, or 57,000 British people.

Most of the missing were arrested during the months that immediately followed Iraq's invasion as the Iraqi security service, the *Mukhabarat*, sought to quell Kuwaiti resistance. Others were taken later as hostages during the run-up to Iraq's retreat. This is no simple list of "missing persons" lost in the confusion of war; 90 percent of the 605 names on the current records are documented by the International Committee of the Red Cross (ICRC) as people being held prisoner. It could be that some of the missing are dead, but I believe that most are being held as a card for Iraq to play at future date.

After the war, Sheikh Salem Al-Sabah set up the Committee for the Kuwaiti Missing and Prisoners of War. Its sole objective is to seek their release and to find out exactly what has happened to the prisoners and, if dead, to claim their remains, which should be returned according to the Geneva Convention. The leadership of Sheikh Salem Al-Sabah has been remarkable. No stone has been left unturned. No world leader has been left in any doubt about the importance that Kuwait attaches to its families, be it President Clinton or President Yeltsin. Baroness Thatcher and President Bush have moved heaven and earth at his behest to bring about some action. In truth, this is unfinished business.

The question is, where do we go from here? Give up? How can you possibly negotiate with a regime run by Saddam Hussein? A more powerful example of evil is hard to find.

For those who have met and come to know the families left behind, this is just not an option. Children have grown up without fathers, wives in reality become widows, some of them desperately young and just beginning their married life when their husbands were taken. Remarriage is quite out of the question. Mothers are distraught. To abandon those facing such a future – be they prisoners or their families – is not acceptable. The world talks about human rights. These prisoners have rights, and they have the right to have every possible avenue pursued in seeking their release. They are not criminals, in fact most of them were not even soldiers.

Through the Foreign Secretary Robin Cook, the British Government has declared an ethical policy that underlines all their dealings with overseas states. It has to be said this was the policy of past governments, but today, the policy has been given a fresh touch of paint. It would certainly be helpful to all of us to learn what fresh initiatives the Government is taking in this regard. The challenge is daunting. It is not one that frightens Sheikh Salem Al-Sabah, who keeps up the momentum of pressure despite his new responsibilities. But we should recognize the obstacles that have to be surmounted.

For a start, the Iraqis deny holding the prisoners. But the Baghdad regime has also denied detaining Iranian prisoners held since the Iran–Iraq War. Under the auspices of the ICRC, the Iraqis have met with the Kuwaiti representatives 51 times in Geneva. The results are frustrating. The Iraqi delegation does not have the power to take any action save procrastination. However, at least they have agreed to the existence of 126 files of Kuwaitis taken to Iraq – but apparently these have been "lost" in the desert in the process.

So frustrating has all this been that the ICRC now wants to abandon their neutral stance supervising and chairing the meetings, and instead implement a new mechanism giving themselves a more proactive role. This would apply to the meetings of the Technical Committee who meet bimonthly on the border. That is also bogged down.

The ICRC has recommended that 45 cases with the best documentation – and the most difficult to refute – be put forward for discussion as a pilot project. After seven long years of cat and mouse games, why, you may wonder, does the Committee persevere? What drives them? The answer is their profound belief, which I share, that there are Kuwaiti prisoners still alive.

This is based on regular intelligence coming forth as a result of every release of a prisoner from an Iraqi jail, Pakistani, Egyptian and even English. As soon as they get home, they are debriefed by a representative from the Prisoners of War (POWs) Committee, often by its very capable and experienced Director, Dr. Duaij Al Anzi. It goes without saying that he has spent a lot of time over the years debriefing Iranians. They all, without fail, tell the same story. Kuwaiti prisoners are known to be in the jails. Word spreads: sometimes they have been seen in an exercise yard, but contact is rarely made for they are kept in separate quarters and moved frequently.

Hopes have been raised recently by the release in early April 1998 of 318 Iranian POWs whom Saddam Hussein has long claimed he did not hold, including the celebrated case of General Hossein Lashkari who had been incarcerated for 18 years. Nobody had any idea that he was even alive. His experiences were horrific – torture, manacles, solitary confinement and constant movement from one house or jail to another. Others tell similar stories.

They tell of being held alone in tiny cells measuring one and a half square meters. Conversation was impossible but they would leave messages for the next prisoner by scratching notes on the walls, giving names and information. Their condition on release was understandably very poor: barely able to stand, very stunted physically and fearful at first of saying too much in case they were not returned to their families after all. For those who remain prisoners, we all fear that the Iraqis may have tested their chemical and biological weapons on them, in short, made guinea pigs of the prisoners. We will never know for sure because the Red Cross is consistently refused access to the prisons.

Certainly Britain, one of the Gulf states' oldest allies, has a moral duty to strive to the utmost to put pressure on the Iraqis to release the prisoners. This must be done through lobbying all our friends and allies. No nation is too small nor too great to take an interest. The United Nations has a key role to play.

We must ensure that sanctions are not lifted until we have full compliance with the relevant UN resolutions especially 686 and 687 at the conclusion of the Gulf War. We are however faced with heavy and highly skilled emotional blackmail by Saddam Hussein, who has been distorting the issue by calling for sympathetic help with providing food and medicines for his people. Labour MP George Galloway drew heavy publicity – indeed it could be interpreted as favorable propaganda – for the Iraqis by flying out a little girl, Mariam, for treatment in a British hospital.

Before we get carried away, we should bear in mind that all along, save for a short period, Saddam Hussein had the power to exchange oil for food and medicines. But when they do arrive, a great portion ends up in the pockets of his officials while the rest piles up undistributed. The plight of the Iraqi people is due to their own leader, not the international community. Matters are not helped by the tremendous pressure applied by nations such as France and Russia who wish to start trading again with Iraq.

It is important that the international community remain clear-eyed. Human rights come before trade. Human rights include the right of illegally held prisoners to be released and sent home to their families or, in the case of death, that their families receive their remains.

I trust that those attending this Conference will remain resolute in their support for a highly important cause which could ultimately affect any one of their countries should they ever have the misfortune to suffer the same plight as Kuwait.

6

GCC Defense Cooperation with the West: A Bahraini Perspective

HH Sheikh Salman Bin Hamed
Bin Eissa Al-Khalifa

May I begin by offering my sincere thanks to His Highness Lieutenant General Sheikh Muhammad bin Zayed Al Nahyan, Chief-of-Staff of the United Arab Emirates Armed Forces, for his kind invitation and may I also commend His Highness for the wise initiative in holding this vitally important conference which unites so many distinguished participants.

This conference comes at a time of critical importance for the Gulf region. A security policy is like a machine; it consists of many separate parts all of which must work together in harmony to achieve the maximum output. To develop a security policy for the region, it is vital to recognize the strengths and weaknesses of the existing defense cooperation arrangements, reflect upon past achievements and anticipate future developments. The State of Bahrain recalls its longstanding friendship with the West and, taking into account the many years of successful and carefully built partnership, wishes to share its perspective and vision of the Gulf Co-operation Council's (GCC) future defense cooperation with the West.

Bahrain believes that it has always maintained a unique position with regard to the West's involvement in the Gulf. The role that it now plays in Western power projections in the region is the result of Bahrain's long-term planning and foresightedness, although its position may have often appeared markedly different from those adopted by others. It was only as a result of the tragic events of 1990-91 that similar cohesive policies of cooperation came to be pursued by other states. However, even then, not all have offered the same level and consistency of support.

Bahrain considers itself to have been the nucleus of the region's strategic defense from as far back as 1820 (with the signing of the first treaty with the British Government) straight through until the end of the 1970s. Bahrain has always been a cornerstone of Western involvement in the region, particularly in the fields of trade and commerce. In the early years of oil exploration, it was Bahrain that provided the bridgehead for British and American survey efforts in the region.

Throughout the twentieth century, Bahrain has adhered to ideals and principles recognized in the "free world," utterly rejecting so-called revolutionary ideologies such as Communism, Fascism or Nazism. Bahrain suffered economically and physically for this commitment, enduring an Italian air raid in 1942 and Communist activities directed against Bahrain with the end of the Marxist Dhofar Rebellion in the mid-1970s. Throughout this period, Bahrain continued to be at the forefront of the Gulf and its links with the West.

In the latter half of the century, Bahrain became the forward operating base for the defense of the Gulf, and Bahrain's defense policy came to be entwined with the needs of the West's protective policies towards the Arabian Peninsula. Bahrain was the bulwark to thwart Iraq's ambitions in 1961 when Abdul Karim Qasim assembled his forces on the Iraq–Kuwait border ready to invade. Bahrain, responding to a request from the Kuwaiti Government, quickly realized how critical the situation was and, despite the reaction of the majority of the Arab world, allowed British forces to deploy in the country. Bahrain supported Kuwait when Iraq repeated the same exercise in 1973, and also stood with Kuwait during the "re-flagging" tanker operations and the associated mine-sweeping campaign that followed.

In 1990, Bahrain became a major coordination center of the coalition efforts to liberate Kuwait. Despite the swift Iraqi occupation of Kuwait, the long-standing cooperation between the West and the GCC, particularly Bahrain, enabled massive mobilization, preparation and logistical support to be accomplished smoothly and with minimum delay. During the war, more than 350 aircraft were deployed in Bahrain. In addition to being a major air operational base, another significant Bahraini contribution to the war effort was its provision of facilities to conduct the naval campaign. The total number of personnel deployed in Bahrain exceeded 20,000 and the wounded were evacuated to the field hospitals which had been erected to provide a capacity of more than 6000 beds. Iraqi missiles targeted Bahrain, though fortunately with no casualties. Total costs incurred by Bahrain to support the war effort were estimated to be US$2.1 billion in tangible costs and approximately US$7.2 billion in non-tangible costs.

Since the liberation, Bahrain has always stood with its GCC neighbors to resist further Iraqi aggression, in particular during Vigilant Warrior in October 1994. In this regard, Bahrain has closely cooperated with and supported the West's efforts to deter Iraq. Bahrain was the first Gulf country to host a US Air Expeditionary Force (AEF) in October 1995. The AEF was then a new concept, introduced in support of Operation Southern Watch, and regarded as a "gap-filler" for the temporary absence of a US aircraft carrier in the Gulf region. Furthermore, Bahrain has hosted additional consecutive AEF deployments, including the first ever deployment of B-1 strategic bombers, to the region. Over the last two years, Bahrain has hosted four of the seven AEF deployments to the region. In addition, to support Operation Southern Watch, Bahrain has allowed Royal Air Force (RAF) tanker aircraft to operate from its international airport and has received several deployments of RAF Nimrod aircraft as well.

Bahrain's commitment to the enforcement of UN resolutions on Iraq also led to its hosting of United Nations Special Commission on Iraq (UNSCOM) Field Office with the additional logistical support which this entails.

In the light of Bahrain's strategic importance and its historical commitment in supporting the defense of not only its own values and interests in the region but also those of its neighbors and the West, it is of no surprise to see the United States Navy's regional operations centered in Bahrain. Since the establishment of the Gulf Area Command on January 1949, the US–Bahrain security relationship has evolved and deepened, despite intense pressure from some quarters for Bahrain to sever these ties.

Bahrain has allowed the Allied Naval Forces Central Europe (NAVCENT) Fifth Fleet Headquarters to move ashore, creating one of the most advanced command and communications centers in the region. The center is certainly considered as the forward operating element for US Central Command (CENTCOM). In addition, in 1997 Bahrain approved a substantial US multi-million dollar expansion of the Administrative Support Unit in Southwest Asia.

In short, prior to the Gulf War, Bahrain provided the largest commitment to the West's power projection efforts and, in support of the war effort, the second largest after Saudi Arabia. Such a high level of commitment from such a small state might come as a surprise to an outside observer. However, those familiar with the history of Bahrain and the Gulf would find nothing unusual about this. Nonetheless, this support has sometimes exerted a heavy toll on Bahrain and caused distractions at times when unity was essential. That is why Bahrain believes it is crucial that all GCC states provide the required support, on an equal basis, so we can achieve and maintain the security of the Gulf. Because of Bahrain's past experiences and support, we feel we have the insight to review defense cooperation with the West.

In recognizing and appreciating the sacrifices and efforts made by Bahrain, it has been possible to see clearly the past level of collective commitment between the West and the GCC. Bahrain believes that we have been reactive for too long and that the initiative should now be seized to plan effectively together, so as to benefit fully from all political and military efforts and achieve a common strategic objective; an objective that will be supported by the international community in general, and the Arab world in particular.

The GCC was established to build a common policy that would achieve and maintain Gulf security. To reach a single overall policy, obstacles in the path of GCC unity must be overcome. Hence, we need to address and realize the issues that cause disunity and disrupt development, and set in motion practical efforts to overcome them.

To analyze any cooperation, we start by looking at the elements that constitute the alliance. The GCC states, as one of the parties involved, must, as HH Sheikh Salem Al-Sabah said, continue to improve the military cooperation among themselves before they can seek to cooperate with the West as a whole. We believe that there are two major obstacles in the path of GCC unity.

The first obstacle is that GCC states perceive and prioritize threats differently: whether by type, size, intention or even source. This obstacle must be addressed internally by the GCC but also with help, whenever appropriate, from the West.

The second obstacle is border disputes. Britain had realized a vacuum would be created by its withdrawal from the Gulf in the early

1970s. However, Britain did not resolve the outstanding border disputes at the time of its withdrawal, believing that the GCC states are capable of solving their own border problems. But I believe that the West and, indeed, the international community, cannot afford to stand by and let outstanding border disputes ferment by adopting policies that preclude involvement. It is worth remembering that Iran invaded islands belonging to the United Arab Emirates because of unresolved territorial issues and now has the ability to threaten the freedom of navigation in the Gulf. The Iran–Iraq War took place as a result of territorial claims and, of course, such a claim was one of the root causes of the Iraqi invasion of Kuwait. Bahrain believes that a more productive role by the West is vital now to help remove the seeds of future conflict.

Bahrain also feels that Western countries are in disagreement as to what role each country must play in this vital region, and there is also disagreement on the actual objectives they are trying to achieve. The recent UN–Iraq standoff is a particular example. We believe that the absence of a common strategic objective was the cause of disharmony between the Western states. We all learned from the Gulf War that, in order to bring together and unite the international community, we must have an overall goal acceptable to all parties. That is why Bahrain believed that further military confrontation with Iraq was a last resort. This belief was based on the following premises:

- that a politically premature military strike could have been counter-productive and could have provided the Iraqi regime with greater external support rather than achieving the intended objective of weakening and deterring it.
- that allowing more time for diplomatic efforts may have brought about the necessary level of international consensus to produce a unified stand with which to face the Iraqi regime.

In brief, Bahrain believed that the optimal way to peacefully solve this crisis, when there was no clear international or Arab mandate for the use of force, was through sustained diplomatic efforts, backed by military pressure, while concurrently achieving international consensus to deny Iraq the opportunity to exploit any perceived differences in the positions of the GCC states towards the use of force.

If this was not done, there were three possible consequences:

- It could have provided excuses for further breaches of applicable Security Council Resolutions, and military action would have lost its legitimacy.
- Iraq would have continued its intransigence.
- A rift with unknown ramifications could have occurred, not only on the Arab front, where solidarity with the suffering of the Iraqi people and sometimes with the Iraqi regime itself was growing, but also within the GCC and its front-line efforts to face the Iraqi regime.

Therefore, it is vital that the West first reaches a consensus on the required course of action before attempting to reach a joint and credible political understanding with the GCC states.

From the beginning, the West's military cooperation with the region was designed to defend the Arabian Peninsula and the Gulf region and to protect the vital interests of the West.

Any cooperation requires a framework. The existing defense agreements, even if initially only bilateral, are the proper tools for formalizing the process of cooperation. The West, as well as the GCC states, must be committed to the defense of the Arabian Peninsula and the West's vital interests. Initial consultation followed by the use of force is an acceptable mechanism only if the initial consultation is taken seriously by all. We should consult immediately whenever a GCC state is threatened but similarly, there must be instantaneous consultation when force is needed to defend the West's vital interests. Bahrain believes this last element has often been lacking. Adhering to this concept will serve the national interests of all, and adherence is best provided for by a clear agreed policy for the use of force. Commitment to initial consultations will allow us to avoid dilemmas arising over the use of force, such as those witnessed in the recent UN–Iraq standoff.

I wish also to raise two issues that are incidental to the GCC's defense cooperation with the West, but which are, nevertheless, of paramount importance when considering the effectiveness of our partnership. They are considerations relating to the peace process and the provision of a joint strategy to combat terrorism.

Bahrain joins with all the GCC states in welcoming the recent initiatives to put the Middle East Peace Process back on track. The peace process is a strategic option for the GCC as well as the entire region. That is why it is vital that the defense cooperation between the GCC and the West must not contradict the current efforts to save the peace process or any other future initiatives or developments. On the contrary, it must support and enhance such efforts. In particular, UN resolutions should be respected and applied evenly and should not be undermined by perceived bias. A further objective of our efforts should be mutual understanding by all concerned of the need to work towards establishing a Middle East that is free from all weapons of mass destruction. These efforts must encompass all states with such capabilities.

Bahrain, as well as other states represented here today, has been tragically affected by terrorism. Today's terrorists have many faces, some of which might be acceptable to a few in the West and they are capable of skillfully using the global media and modern technology to their greatest advantage. Bahrain's experience is that international cooperation is a prerequisite to ensuring that the terrorists cannot organize, operate or publicize their crimes. This is vital to achieving justice. No safe haven can be provided for terrorists, their supporters or fronts, and active and open dialogue between the concerned authorities in the GCC and the West is long overdue. Indeed, if action is not taken, it is the West's interests that will be threatened in the long term. The scenario of a biological weapon in a suitcase is disturbing, to say the least.

I hope I have provided today a brief insight into Bahrain's position regarding the future security of the Gulf region. My country is committed to ensuring the effectiveness and readiness of the GCC to face external aggression with one voice. We recognize the need for and welcome cooperation with the West, but remain concerned that much still needs to be done to cement and build further upon the foundation already laid.

7

Energy Security in the Gulf

HE Mr. Hisham Nazer

In our present world where political, economic and cultural insularity have been eroded by distance, where time and space no longer handcuff human communication, and where the time-cherished concept of sovereignty is considered anachronistic in international affairs, security must be redefined within the parameters of these operational factors. It is time, therefore, to consider the fallacies surrounding the issue of energy security.

Conventional wisdom had it that energy security relates first and foremost to that of the West (i.e., North America and Western Europe) with the rest of the world assuming second place; this is not without reason. In 1996, the West consumed some 32 million barrels a day of refined products, or 48 percent of world consumption. Its whole modern civilization, economic growth and military prowess are based on the perpetual energy generation of which oil would probably constitute 41 percent by the year 2000. The West has always been a producer of energy, including crude oil, but its domestic sources are either being depleted or are unable to quench its consumptive appetite. Its current reserves are about 55 billion barrels, which at current consumption levels will be enough for only five years. The West is also a producer of alternative energy sources that could prove viable in the future. But until that happens, and until alternative energy can economically supply all consumption sectors, it will have to rely on imports, most conspicuously from the Gulf. North America and Western Europe currently import almost 20 million barrels of oil a day.

It is also true that other areas in the world which may seem more accommodating to the West at the moment have satisfactory oil reserves. Latin America holds about 138 billion barrels; Eastern Europe, including Russia, accounts for about 60 billion barrels, and Africa approximately 76 billion barrels. All countries in these areas are experiencing economic growth which may increase domestic consumption and reduce exports. Each area has its own local and international political and economic problems, and security issues change with changing circumstances. Yet, what makes these countries more reliable as oil suppliers than countries in the Gulf area?

On the surface, therefore, it seems that the other side of the security equation has it all. Were we to consider Iran as a member of the Gulf community, as we should, then the Gulf sits firmly on the vastest and most valuable resource in history. Together, the Gulf region accounts for over 670 billion barrels of reserves or 84 percent of known recoverable oil reserves. Some of those countries annually discover more than they produce and export, therefore maintaining seemingly undiminishing reserve levels. Additionally when exports were partially halted from the Gulf, oil prices quadrupled, causing serious hardship to the economies of many countries. The reason why the world was able to cope with the temporary cessation of exports from Iraq and Iran during their war was because other Gulf countries were able to immediately fill the gap with their excess capacity. Yet, under current circumstances, any sizable reduction in exports from the Gulf for a sustainable period of time could cause serious economic dislocation.

Therefore, oil supplies are very important for the West. In essence, that means that oil must continue to be explored, developed, produced, refined, transported and made available to consumers through commercial outlets at reasonable prices. Each of such generalities enumerated here has a specific definition in the minds of Western policy makers. For example, the producing countries in the Gulf mostly carry out their own exploration for oil. The West would prefer this process to be done through concession agreements in the spirit of the 1920s and 1930s wherein consumers have a say and some control. They continue to pursue that objective by various means. We should not be surprised if, in the future, some global scheme in the name of the environment is devised through the United Nations or some other international agency to secure access to resources that are vital for world economy. It could materialize through the new corridors of globalism, free trade or market democracy.

I do not propose to get into that for the purposes of this discussion. Yet the fact remains that the figures I mentioned above are very unsettling for the West. We constantly hear unabashed statements that a security objective of Western countries in particular and industrial countries in general is to reduce dependence on foreign oil, specifically Gulf oil. They have energetically taken great strides in that direction.

The West created the International Energy Agency as a dynamic answer to the oil crisis of the 1970s. In 1996, the estimated commercial stocks on land amounted to around 2.4 billion barrels of oil, enough for 62 days of consumption for Organisation for Economic Co-operation and Development (OECD) countries at current levels. Strategic reserves are some 1.2 billion barrels of oil, enough for 30 days of consumption. Added together, stocks and strategic reserves were 3.6 billion barrels, which would carry OECD countries through for 92 days until any oil crisis would be resolved. It has been reported recently that there is a remorselessly rising tide of crude stocks in OECD member countries. Total commercial stocks increased in February 1998 over February 1997 by some 591,000 barrels per day to reach 5.9 billion barrels. Additionally, a system of oil supply sharing is in place during an oil supply crisis, which would certainly alleviate some of the pressure on the members in case of supply disruptions. No Gulf country can withstand any impediments to its exports for a comparable period of time, especially with the dilution of their currency reserves. At their current expenditure levels, it is unlikely that reserves will return to the levels of the 1970s and 1980s.

Furthermore, Gulf countries, whether friendly or unfriendly to the West, are aware of the aircraft carriers, cruise missiles and smart bombs close to their shores. They also know that even a catastrophic event such as the burning of oil wells, as happened in Kuwait during the Gulf War, may not be as disastrous as was first thought. Supplies were replaced more efficiently that it was thought possible, and the wells themselves were restored and put back into production in a remarkably short time.

When punishment is necessary, sanctions are imposed. There are currently three oil-producing countries, two of them in the Gulf area, under some form of international or individual sanctions. Both Iraq and Iran are currently unable to produce their quotas as approved by the United Nations or allotted by the Organization of Petroleum Exporting Countries (OPEC) due to the lack of equipment and technology. Additionally, the fall in income and the huge impact these sanctions have inflicted on the people of those countries are yet to be measured. We are now witnessing an embargo in reverse, by consumers on producers rather than by producers on consumers.

The West has also made great strides in reducing the cost of producing oil in Western fields, increasing recovery ratios and stretching the longevity of their reserves. Early expectations that the North Sea oil field would soon be depleted have not materialized. On the contrary, production increased from 2.1 million barrels a day in 1980 to 5.8 million barrels a day in 1996, surpassing all the oil producers in the Gulf area except Saudi Arabia.

From the geopolitical point of view, oil is the coveted commodity that all countries fight to obtain. Cynics would be reluctant to accept the altruistic reasons for the 1990 Gulf War – that it was fought to uphold the will of the international community, to protect national sovereignties and the rule of law. They would point to the fact that there was, and there still is plenty of oil in the area of conflict which needs to be protected. No conflict could have created an alliance of such diverse countries and old adversaries had it not been for the paramount importance of the commodity at stake.

It is true that just before the Gulf War another war was raging between Iraq and Iran, two major producing countries in the area, with nobody making any attempt, individually or internationally, to end the hostilities. In that particular instance, it was said, there was no imminent danger to oil supplies to the world market. In fact, a situation existed the likes of which had never previously been experienced in the arena of human conflict. Both countries were not what the West would consider on its list of friends. For most of the war, both countries were attacking each other while producing and exporting oil at the same time. Other countries in the area had enough capacity not only to supplant any production shortfalls by those two countries, but they were also spending huge sums on arms purchases from the West. It was thought that when both countries lost the stamina to continue the conflict, and recognized their need for peace without foreign encouragement, both would need to rebuild and repair the destruction they had caused each other. Western companies and western technology would be needed to implement the reconstruction.

It is not too unrealistic, therefore, to construe from all this that the West has more time on its hands to feel secure about oil supplies until new sources of supply are found and harnessed, or alternative energy sources are developed and made economically viable. In the meantime, policies are pursued diligently to reduce consumption at all levels. Two such policies seem to be much more conspicuously pursued with measurable success.

First, the issue of domestic taxation on oil consumption has been of serious concern to oil producers in the Gulf area. In 1996, the composite barrels of oil which were valued at US$20.50 (cost, insurance and freight) in Italian ports was sold in Italian markets for US$114. Of that price, US$77.20 were taxes. The average income per barrel for Gulf producers was no more than US$20 a barrels in 1996, one of the best years in recent history. Also, taxes on oil more than doubled in Italy between 1986 and 1996, rising from US$36.30 a barrel to US$77.20 a barrel. The same could be said for almost all Western countries. In France, a composite barrel which was sold in French markets in 1996 for US$120.60 comprised US$83.40 in taxes. In Germany, of US$105.20 per barrel sold, taxes reached US$63.50, and in the UK, US$69 were taxes in a price of US$112.60. Consumer country governments in Western Europe make in taxes on a barrel of oil almost four times as much as the countries who produce and transport that oil to them.

Taxes reduce demand to the detriment of oil producers. In fact, no Western country endorses lower prices to its citizens. Lower prices run the risk of higher taxes at the pump, an irony most Western consumers fail to recognize. Dr. Lukman, OPEC Secretary General, estimated that in 1996 four major oil consumers – Japan, Germany, Canada and the United States – received more income from their taxes on oil than the 11 OPEC member countries earned from their total oil exports. When France, Italy and the United Kingdom are added, making up the G7, they received 70 percent more oil tax revenue than OPEC earned from oil exports.

The second issue is that of the environment, a noble cause harboring questionable motives. There are basically three environmental problems often cited in relation to the use of fossil fuels and the emission of greenhouse gases such as carbon monoxide. The first questions whether a problem exists at all. The notion that excessive emissions of greenhouse gases cause catastrophic climate change is believed by some scientists to be a non-problem, and best ignored. The proponents of this argument base their opinion on the fact that climate-change scenarios were based on computer modeling that is not related to reality. Additionally, the role of solar activity on global temperature has not been resolved since there is no empirical evidence to suggest a relationship between the two. Unless scientific evidence proves beyond a reasonable doubt that the emission of greenhouse gases causes climate change, political decisions that would impact on economic development, especially of developing countries, would be ill-advised. It would be politically difficult to reverse policies based on erroneous information today which may be proved wrong in the future. The environment argument is proving a successful vehicle for political ends, both on the domestic and international fronts, but should not be permitted to continue in that direction.

The second view is that there is unreasonable and uneven emphasis on fossil fuels in relation to other pollutants. More and more countries are imposing taxes on oil and its products while ignoring nuclear energy and subsidizing coal. Deforestation and desertification receive less attention, and poverty, the primary pollutant of the earth, is almost ignored. If fossil fuels do prove to be responsible for polluting the earth, then tax money should be spent on research to produce clean products rather than on unrelated issues.

Third, it has been argued that the impact of taxes should not be seen only in relation to its suppression of demand, and thereby the need to compensate the oil producers for the loss of income. That argument, as valid as it may seem and as legally supported as it is by the Convention on Climate Change, would not generate international sympathy or objective analysis. Rather, it should be explained in terms of its impact on the development of the oil industry itself. Lower income reduces the ability of producers to invest in exploration and development of new fields, or increase capacity when the market indicates growth in consumption, or research and develop new technologies to produce more environment-friendly products. Dr. Likman estimated that if the OECD imposed a uniform carbon tax of US$300 per ton on 1996 prices, OPEC countries would lose around US$600 billion in cumulative revenues over a 25-year period between 1995 and 2020. The impact on world energy security would be critical. Given the long lead-time needed in oil developments, the world would face sudden and inflationary hikes in energy prices.

Gulf countries, like other oil producers in OPEC and elsewhere, should be wary of promises. In December 1997, there was an attempt to drag developing countries into voluntarily accepting future emission limits, when the Berlin Mandate clearly waived new commitments for developing countries. However, they are not yet as safe as they think they are. US Vice President Al Gore vowed after the Kyoto conference in 1997 to get developing nations to accept emission limits before seeking Senate ratification.

The West could, however, upset the scales which seem to favor them at the present. Foreign policy duplicity regarding the peace process and weapons of mass destruction in the area, the race to sell arms at the expense of economic and social development, the attempt to superimpose Western concepts of democracy and human rights on societies which have their own concepts of governance and human rights would only lead to rage, which would ultimately lead to conflict and violence. We have already seen signs of the looming tempest during the attempt to militarily enforce Security Council resolutions on Iraq, while the faltering enforcement of the already-signed Oslo Agreement was met with impotence.

It would be sad, indeed, if violence in any form flares up in the area, stirring its seemingly calm waters. Gulf countries should be the least susceptible to instability. These are countries that are endowed with huge natural resources and relatively small populations. They are countries with strong spiritual affiliation, well-knit social fabric, and a geographic location which affords them Eastern and Western affinities. They are eager to develop both economically and politically. When they commenced their modern development in the early 1970s, they attracted the attention of the whole world to the way they planned it, the way they implemented it and the way they maneuvered around its pitfalls. They have become modern societies with their own redesigned institutions and their eagerness to contribute to human civilization. They believe they can handle their own local problems if they are left alone to evolve, merely by exercising the human will to change.

It is historically true, however, that no course of human development is totally devoid of problems. There will always be obstacles to human progress. All forms of dictatorship and totalitarianism can develop, and the Gulf is no exception. But these will wither away like all forms of oppression have throughout history, and the human affinity for change will prevail. But when Western intentions in the area reflect only the desire to reap the greatest benefits in the shortest possible time irrespective of the impact on the future welfare of the people of the area, when duplicity in Western policies is evident, and when the West tries to superimpose a mono-culture on the area without the necessary receptiveness on the part of its people, that would be a direct invitation to the tornadoes of instability.

On their part, Gulf countries should not wholly react to Western policies, but should take charge of their own destiny. In the area of energy, they should accommodate changing circumstances by changing their direction. They should recognize that at present they are much more vulnerable than the West in the area of energy security. In the 1970s when the West was confronted with shortage in oil supplies, they reacted in an intelligent way; they reduced their consumption. About 6.5 million barrels a day were lost forever to producers in OPEC, mostly Gulf countries, by those Western policies. Similarly, the only way to reduce the glut in the demand is to decrease expenditure by Gulf governments. Their need for income would be reduced, thereby eliminating cut-throat competition for market share.

Gulf countries must reject being singled out as the villains of the oil trade. They shoulder more than their fair share of world energy problems. Their global energy cooperation should not be restricted to the narrow scope of OPEC action. They should lead the way in changing OPEC into an oil-producing organization where all producing countries of the world can be persuaded to work together in developing technology to reduce the cost of production and to refine clean products, rather than be led into a future with no prospects.

Until that happens, every attempt should be made by Gulf countries to penetrate all markets wherever possible, specifically, by buying marketing assets or creating joint venture marketing entities in heavily populated areas such as China and India, and high growth potential countries such as South East Asia and the United States. They should also create more direct and energetic contact with all developing countries in the hope of establishing a constituency strong enough to impede the implementation of all international agreements adverse to their interests. In fact, they should not ignore the highly industrialized countries of Western Europe and the Western hemisphere but should try to cooperate with these countries for the common good of both.

Gulf countries must understand clearly that energy security is reciprocal. Their policy should reflect neither accommodation nor confrontation. It should reflect assertion.

Concluding Remarks

Dr. Jamal S. Al-Suwaidi

On behalf of His Highness Lieutenant General Sheikh Muhammad Bin Zayed Al-Nahyan, Chief-of-Staff of the UAE Armed Forces, I would like to express my warmest appreciation and gratitude to all the esteemed participants in this Gulf Security conference.

The past two days have proven to be highly productive both in terms of the thoughtful and provocative presentations that have been given as well as the rich discussion periods that followed.

Various strategic- and defense-related issues that will determine the future security of the Gulf with relation to British policy have been considered and insightfully discussed, in addition to the integral role that the GCC–UK relationship will play in the security equation. The ability to reach a solid understanding and engage in a productive exchange of views is a central component to this issue, especially in terms of cementing the already strong relations existing between the Gulf Co-operation Council and the United Kingdom. Equally important is the ability to create a mutual base of awareness on which a more stable and broader security policy framework for the Gulf region can be built and successfully maintained.

Allow me to touch briefly upon some of the main themes that have emerged from the conference presentations and their discussions. An unstable regional security balance does not only provide for a near-term military threat, it also puts in jeopardy the overall human, social and cultural development of the Arab Gulf region and the tremendous advances that have been achieved so far. Ultimately, only a stable indigenous security paradigm that is primarily defined by national and regional interests will be able effectively to guarantee overcoming the current inherent instability. In order to foster such understanding, the GCC needs to be able to call upon the assistance and support of its allies and to put to use its long-standing historical relationship with the United Kingdom in order to establish a more peaceful and stable security environment.

It should also be increasingly clear that security can no longer be referred to exclusively within its military context. Economic prosperity, social and cultural well-being are factors that increasingly define the security of a nation's population, which makes their inclusion in the development of effective and responsive public policies essential. It has to be an imperative to avoid military hostilities while at the same time diversifying economies, developing stronger trading relationships and increasing economic integration. Here the traditional perimeter mentality needs to be expanded in order to allow for evolutionary instead of revolutionary change as well as to increase the economic stakes within the system so that the interests of all the actors involved becomes directly tied to maintaining the safety and security of the system as a whole.

As has been done during this conference, the topic of Gulf security needs to be approached with an open mind and an objective set of criteria from which one can proceed.

I would like to take this opportunity to extend my thanks and express my deep gratitude for Your Highnesses' and Your Excellencies' honorable attendance, which has made this conference a most interesting and productive event.

Contributors

HH Sheikh Salman Bin Hamed Bin Eissa Al-Khalifa
His Highness Sheikh Salman is currently the Under-Secretary of Defense for the State of Bahrain as well as the Chairman of the Board of Trustees of the Bahrain Center for Studies and Research. In 1994 he obtained an MPhil from Queen's College, Cambridge. From 1988 to 1995, His Highness was part of the Bahrain Defense Force Reserves as a Second Lieutenant to Captain. In 1992, he was appointed Deputy Chairman of the Board of Trustees of the Bahrain Center for Studies and Research until 1995, when he assumed his current position as Chairman of the Board of Trustees.

HH Sheikh Salem Sabah Al-Salem Al-Sabah
His Highness Sheikh Salem was appointed Deputy Prime Minister and Minister of Defense for the State of Kuwait in 1996 and, since 1991, Deputy Prime Minister and Minister of Foreign Affairs. Currently, he is also Head of the National Committee for Kuwaiti Prisoners of War and Missing Persons. Between 1961 and 1965, His Highness served as Head of the Legal Department at the Ministry of Foreign Affairs, after which he headed the Political Department in the same Ministry. Between 1965 and 1971, he was appointed Ambassador of the State of Kuwait to the United Kingdom during which time he also served as a non-resident Ambassador for Kuwait to Sweden, Norway and Denmark. In 1971, he became the Ambassador to the United States and non-resident Ambassador to Canada and Venezuela. His Highness Sheikh Salem has also served in several Ministerial positions prior to his current position. In 1975, he served as Minister for Labor and Social Affairs, followed by his appointment as Minister of Defense from 1978 to 1988. He then occupied the position of Minister of the Interior until 1991.

Dr. Jamal S. Al-Suwaidi is Director of the Emirates Center for Strategic Studies and Research in Abu Dhabi, United Arab Emirates (UAE) and Professor at the UAE University in Al Ain. He has taught courses in political methodology, political culture, comparative governments and international relations at the UAE University and the University of Wisconsin.

Dr. Al-Suwaidi earned his MA and PhD degrees in Political Science at the University of Wisconsin-Milwaukee and his BS degree in Political Science at Kuwait University. He is the author of numerous articles on a variety of topics including perceptions of democracy in Arab and Western societies, women and development, and UAE public opinion on the Gulf crisis. Dr. Al-Suwaidi is author of "Gulf Security and the Iranian Challenge," *Security Dialogue* vol. 27, no. 3 (1996); a contributing author to *Democracy, War and Peace in the Middle East*; editor of *The Yemeni War: Causes and Consequences*, the award-winning *Iran and the Gulf: A Search for Stability*, and *The Gulf Co-operation Council: Prospects for the Twenty-first Century*.

General Sir Charles Guthrie
General Guthrie was appointed Chief of the Defence Staff in April 1997, having served previously as Chief of the General Staff. He was commissioned into the Welsh Guards in 1959 and subsequently served for four years with the Special Air Service (SAS) in Aden, the Gulf, Malaysia and East Africa. He later commanded the First Battalion Welsh Guards in Berlin and Northern Ireland. He became Assistant Chief of General Staff in 1987 and subsequently held a range of senior staff and command appointments including Commander, Northern Army Group and Commander-in-Chief, British Army of the Rhine.

Lady Olga Maitland
Lady Olga Maitland is Head of the UK Committee for Kuwaiti Prisoners of War and Missing Persons in Iraq. While a Member of Parliament from 1992 to 1997, she consistently raised the issue in the House of Commons and campaigned vigorously to draw public attention to the plight of the POWs. In March 1996, she helped the Committee's President Sheikh Salem Al-Sabah, the Defense Minister and Deputy Prime Minister to organize an international conference in London on

the subject which was addressed by President George Bush and Baroness Thatcher. Lady Olga, President of the Defence and Security Forum which she linked up with the Free Kuwait Campaign during the invasion, continues her campaigning as a journalist, writer and broadcaster.

HE Mr. Hisham Nazer

Currently Chairman of the Nazer Group of companies in the Kingdom of Saudi Arabia, His Excellency Mr. Nazer started his career in public services with the Saudi oil sector. In 1961, he became the first Governor to represent his country on the OPEC Board of Governors. He served as Deputy Minister of Petroleum and Mineral Resources from 1962 to 1968.

Named President of the Central Planning Organization (CPO) in 1968, and a member of the Saudi cabinet chaired by King Faisal, he was charged with setting the direction and pace of Saudi Arabia's economic development through a series of five-year plans. When the CPO was succeeded in 1975 by the establishment of an official Ministry, he became its first Minister, and drafted the five-year development plans for Saudi Arabia for the years between 1970 and 1995. In 1986, Mr. Nazer became the Minister of Petroleum and presided over a program to restructure and integrate the Saudi oil sector. In March 1989, he became the first Saudi Chairman of the Board of the newly established Saudi Arabian Oil Company (Saudi Aramco), which is recognized as the world's largest oil company.

Dr. John Reid MP

Dr. Reid is Member of Parliament for Hamilton North and Bellshill and was appointed Minister of State for the Armed Forces in May 1997. He holds a PhD in Economic History. He was elected to Parliament in 1987 and became Shadow Spokesman on Defence in 1995. He has been Joint Vice-Chairman of the All-Party Groups on Azerbaijan, Belize, Russia and Uganda, as well as a member of a range of other All-Party groups. He is a Fellow of the Armed Forces Parliamentary Scheme, having completed a period of secondment to the British Army.

Rt. Hon George Robertson MP

George Robertson is Member of Parliament for Hamilton South and was appointed Secretary of State for Defence after the 1997 General

Election. He became a member of the Opposition Front Bench after the 1979 General Election, first on Scottish Affairs, then on Defence and Foreign Affairs from 1982 to 1993. He was made Deputy Opposition Spokesman for Foreign and Commonwealth Affairs in 1983 and additionally principal Spokesman on European Affairs in 1984. He was elected to the Shadow Cabinet and appointed Shadow Secretary of State for Scotland in 1993. He is a former Chairman of the Scottish Labour Party. He was also Vice-Chairman of the Board of the British Council from 1985 to 1994 and served for seven years on the Council of the Royal Institute of International Affairs. He is a Governor of the Ditchley Foundation.

Index